Playing for Range

PLAYING FOR RANGERS NO19

Edited by Ken Gallacher

Stanley Paul

London Melbourne Auckland Johannesburg

Stanley Paul and Co. Ltd

An imprint of Century Hutchinson Ltd
Brookmount House, 62–65 Chandos Place
Covent Garden, London WC2N 4NW

Century Hutchinson Australia (Pty) Ltd
PO Box 496, 16–22 Church Street, Hawthorn, Melbourne, Victoria 3122

Century Hutchinson New Zealand Limited
191 Archers Road, PO Box 40–086, Glenfield, Auckland 10

Century Hutchinson South Africa (Pty) Ltd
PO Box 337, Bergvlei 2012, South Africa

First published 1987
Copyright © Stanley Paul and Co. Ltd 1987

Set in Baskerville by Deltatype Ltd, Ellesmere Port, South Wirral

Printed and bound in Great Britain by Anchor Brendon Ltd, Tiptree, Essex

British Cataloguing in Publication Data

Playing for Rangers. — No. 19
    1.   Rangers Football Club — Periodicals
    796.334'63'0941443   GV943.6.R3

ISBN 0 09 171311 0

Black and white photographs by Sportapics
Colour photographs by Colorsport

Frontispiece: Goalkeeper Chris Woods rises confidently to hold this cross as Celtic striker Mo Johnston lurks dangerously behind him

CONTENTS

THE TITLE FAMINE ENDS

Thousands of fans invaded the field at Pittodrie on the afternoon of 2 May – and that was the beginning of Rangers' title celebrations. As skipper Terry Butcher and his team-mates disappeared from view as the fans engulfed them, chairman David Holmes must have allowed a quiet smile of satisfaction to play across his face in the directors' box. For this was the moment he had hoped for, the day he had dreamed about since taking over as the club's chief executive little more than a year earlier.

But even Holmes and his player-boss Graeme Souness had not expected to see the nine-year-long title famine end for the Ibrox club in their first season together. This was a bonus for them – just as it was a bonus for the fans, starved of success for so long. They had seen the Scottish Cup and the League Cup appear in the Ibrox Trophy Room, but since 1978 they had not seen the championship flag fly from the stands.

When Souness arrived he made it plain that the title was always his major priority. But, privately, he knew that to take the Premier League championship in his first season as a manager, and in his first season with the club, could be beyond him and his team.

When they won the Skol Cup at the end of October by beating Old Firm rivals Celtic in the Hampden final the Rangers' bosses looked on the victory as a bonus. Perhaps they felt that the team, still being remoulded by Souness, was always going to be a better bet to land a cup rather than a title. There were signs of fragility about the player pool which suggested that. Signs which spelled out that the long, long haul to the title in a forty-four game Premier League would be too great a task for them.

It didn't turn out that way. Instead of the Rangers side cracking under the pressure of going for the championship it was Celtic who wilted in the closing games. The team who were defending the title they had won so dramatically the previous season did beat

One member of the 'Anglo connection' – giant skipper Terry Butcher powering his way past a challenge from Motherwell's Paul Smith

Rangers in the Old Firm clash at Parkhead, and then slipped alarmingly in other games. They dropped a vital point against Dundee United in a game on their own ground. That allowed Rangers a vital edge on the run in, and it was then that Celtic threw away any chances they might still have had.

Mathematically it was always going to be possible for Rangers to win the championship that afternoon at Aberdeen. But even the most diehard fans could not have expected the championship to be decided in the way it was. For as Rangers battled their way to a 1–1 draw with their jinx side Aberdeen, Celtic were going down to a sensational defeat from Falkirk at Parkhead. It was a result which stunned Scottish football, and which gave Rangers their title win.

But, while that Celtic defeat contributed mightily to the celebrations at Pittodrie, it was the gritty display by the Rangers players which made certain that they would be champions.

Player-boss Graeme Souness had been sent off in the first half, before a marvellous header from Terry Butcher gave the Ibrox men the lead. And, even after Aberdeen equalized, the ten-man Rangers side held on grimly and determinedly to take a vital point. Encouraged by the roars from the crowd which told them Celtic were in trouble, they matched the full-strength Aberdeen to hold on for the honourable draw they wanted. Even if they had lost they would still have been champions – but not one of this Rangers team wanted to mark the end of a nine-year wait with a hollow victory. Not one of them wanted to win the flag on a day when they were beaten.

Victory at the ground which has held so many disappointments and defeats down through the Premier League years was still beyond them. But the draw satisfied the players and delighted the fans who spilled over from the terracings when the final whistle sounded. It was the start of the celebrations which continued the next week at Ibrox when Rangers played their last game of the season against the team which was to win the Scottish Cup, St Mirren.

More than forty-three thousand fans were at Ibrox for the party. Tickets had been sold out weeks earlier, and fans were paying black-market prices outside the ground for the few which were available. Inside, the fans roared their delight when Robert Fleck gave them an early goal, and then spent the afternoon singing the praises of their heroes.

When the championship trophy was presented there was a mini-invasion from the enclosure. But then the bulk of the crowd roared their disapproval and soon the players, led by the delighted Butcher, were able to make a triumphant lap of honour.

Another member of that Anglo club – goalkeeper Chris Woods. Here he is with assistant manager Walter Smith, chairman David Holmes and director Freddy Fletcher on the day he joined up at Ibrox

The self-styled 'English connection' of Terry Butcher, Graham Roberts, and Chris Woods took off their jerseys to reveal T-shirts which bore the legend: McButcher or McRoberts or McWoods – the English connection. It underlined again how the three English stars had committed themselves to the club, and how they had forged a special link with the Ibrox support. Suggestions from the south when they signed that Rangers' fans would not take kindly to Englishmen playing for the club had been proved wrong early in the season. Now, with the title won, and the trio of English stars installed among the Ibrox heroes the whole idea that they would be unacceptable was a joke. All three had been welcomed, and

Left: The final vital member of the Ibrox English brigade – iron-man defender Graham Roberts

Right: The man himself, the boss – Graeme Souness with a word of warning for one of his players

Terry Butcher was being talked of in the same breath as Willie Woodburn, one of the greatest centre-halves Rangers had ever had.

In one season chairman Holmes and player-boss Souness had wrought a revolution. They had changed the attitudes of the fans, broadened their horizons and increased the ambitions of the club. They had also been able to guide the team to two trophy victories, and bring the championship back after nine long empty years.

Souness had said when he took over that a club like Rangers should never be without the title for that length of time. He meant it. And he changed it. The Souness era was under way, and one title was never going to be enough to satisfy him. Or the new, ambitious Rangers. They wanted this to be the start of something big. . . .

I'LL DO IT MY WAY
says Graeme Souness

In one year in Scottish soccer Graeme Souness had a greater single impact than anyone since Jock Stein took control of Celtic some twenty years earlier. Then Stein embarked on a run of success which has never been equalled. He led Celtic to a European Cup win – the first ever by a British team – and to nine championship victories in succession. He also built a team which brought dignity and respect back to Scottish soccer.

Now Souness is doing the same thing, but in a different way. Stein performed most of his miracles with home-grown talent, laced with a few players bought from other Scottish clubs. Souness has gone international. His transformation has been even more dramatic than Stein's, a man he admired so much when he was Scotland's captain and Stein, the international team manager.

The Liverpool man audaciously plundered the English transfer market. Two of Bobby Robson's international team are now at Ibrox in skipper Terry Butcher and goalkeeper Chris Woods. The Spurs defender Graham Roberts also turned his back on the First Division to join up at Ibrox, and suddenly Rangers were attracting more interest south of the Border than any Scottish club had ever done before.

All of these moves were down to Souness himself. He was the man who persuaded the players to move into Scottish soccer – and his own example helped. His decision to carry on his career in his native country made others realize that Rangers could become something special. Here the Rangers player-manager explains to Ken Gallacher in an interview how he set about the job, and how he intends to continue the Ibrox success story.

Gallacher: It was a revolutionary step to bring top English players to the Premier League. Why did you take that decision?
Souness: First of all it wasn't a decision simply to bring in top English players. I wanted to bring in *top players* period. The fact that they were English didn't come into it. These were class players who were available and players I knew from the time I had spent in the English First Division with Liverpool.

Also I think that anyone will realize that we found major problems in trying to buy players from Scottish clubs. The first major target for us was my World Cup team-mate Richard Gough who was at Dundee United. We made offers for him and we were turned down by United. They made it very plain that they were not going to sell the player to us. Eventually he went to Tottenham Hotspur, even though we were ready to pay more money to sign him.

There were other instances, too, when it was obvious to us that clubs didn't want to sell their stars to us if we were interested. We made an approach for Craig Levein of Hearts, and the message was the same as the one we received from Tannadice.

By that time I had made up my mind. If Scottish clubs didn't want our money then we would spend the cash elsewhere. The clubs in England had a much more realistic attitude to the whole business of transfers and, then, Europe is a big market as well. Also, we were buying the best players around. Chris Woods is a class goalkeeper, Terry Butcher is the best central defender in Europe for my money, and then Graham Roberts added another vital piece of experience alongside Terry.

Gallacher: Did you find it difficult to persuade the players to come north? After all they had spent their careers in the English First Division and Scottish soccer doesn't always enjoy the best of reputations in the south.

Souness: Admittedly it took some persuasion, but once the season had started, once the players realized just how big the club was, they knew that I hadn't misled them. I told them quite simply that they were coming to a top club – one that was going to go places.

One worry Chris and Terry had was that it might affect their international team places, but the England boss Bobby Robson gave them assurances that it would make no difference. It hasn't, either. In fact Chris has won more caps since joining Rangers than he had before!

By the time Graham joined us he knew the score. He had been up to watch us in the Skol Cup Final and recognized that he was coming on board with a club which was going to make an impact on the game.

Gallacher: He did a lot to add even more backbone to the club didn't he?

Souness: Well, if we had signed him a little bit earlier we might have had a better run in Europe than we managed to have. Graham has

All the single-mindedness and determination that have made Graeme Souness so successful as a player and a manager are shown here in this action shot

A smile on the face of the tiger as Graham Roberts laughs off a challenge which left him grounded. Souness says he knew he had won the title when Roberts joined from Spurs

tremendous experience and he is a winner. I like that. When we signed him and he slotted in so well, that's when I knew we could win the title. He was one of the missing links. Honestly, I believe he should be in the England side. I said that when he signed for us back in December. His partnership with Terry is so effective. If I was Bobby Robson I would have the pair of them playing together for England; I have always felt that club partnerships tend to do well at international level.

Gallacher: When you kicked off on your buying spree a lot of cynics took a look at what was happening and then said that football teams cannot buy their way to success. You've done it – but what do you think of that kind of talk?

Souness: Well, first of all, it depends on which players you buy, doesn't it. If you buy well then obviously you can get success. If you buy badly then you will fail. That's fairly obvious to me.

As to the general theory, it's something that I don't go along with. When I was at Liverpool almost all the players had been bought. There were one or two who had come through from the youth team and the reserves, but they were in a minority during my years at Anfield and I think that situation still exists.

Would you say that Liverpool were unsuccessful? Or, look at Everton. Most of their players have been bought too. In Italy it is the same.

We want to have players coming through the system at Ibrox, but when I took over as manager there were things which needed to be done immediately if we were going to win trophies and bring back the fans. I couldn't wait for a few years for a class centre-half to emerge, or hang around waiting to see if a keeper with Chris Woods' class would arrive. That wasn't possible. The chairman told me that money was available to buy top-class players. He wanted a Rangers team back at the top, and so we took the short cut there. But remember the biggest buys I made were proven international players. I didn't reckon I was gambling by paying out big money for the players I was getting.

Gallacher: You have indicated that you intend to continue with that policy. I mean, that you are going to carry on spending big money on star players.

Souness: Yes, of course I will. Again, I learned at Liverpool that it's no use having piles of money in the bank and maybe have the team struggling a little. Our assets have to be on the park. That's where you find success and that's what the public wants as well. Our fans have responded magnificently and they have to see the best.

Gallacher: While on the subject of the support – how much did you appreciate their backing this season?

Souness: I can't tell you just how much it meant to me and to all of the lads. From the first moment a ball was kicked in earnest until the last kick of that last game against St Mirren at Ibrox they were absolutely magnificent. Even after the Scottish Cup defeat from Hamilton, they didn't desert us. They proved to me and to the other players that we were giving them what they wanted. You only have to look at the gates we had during the season. In ten of our League games we topped forty thousand fans at Ibrox, almost every away game was all ticket. They were absolutely fantastic. And the way they took to the new players was great. I suppose big Terry and the others might have had a little bit of apprehension about how the fans would react to Englishmen playing for the club. Well, they needn't have worried, the fans loved them.

Basically the fans want to see good players in action for the club no matter where they come from. I'll tell you something else I believe – they are paying the money that keeps the club going so it's their money we are spending on players. If we bring top players to the club then it's because the fans have given us the cash to do so. The chairman spelled that out before. The money we make from the gate receipts, especially if we have a successful European run will be ploughed back into the club. We have a debt to the fans and a responsibility to them. Having the best players at the club is one way of repaying them for their loyalty.

Gallacher: Onto a more personal note, now. How did you feel yourself about the season? Was it as hard as you imagined? Or did you find the whole business of playing and managing a top side easier than you might have expected?

Souness: Taking the first question I enjoyed almost every minute of it. There were some disappointments on the playing side and they made me think long and hard about whether I should continue as a player with the club.

Obviously I'm talking about the two orderings off I suffered – at the start of the season and then again at the end. It's still difficult for me to grasp the fact that I was sent off in the very first match. Then, for it to happen again in the second last game was a terrible blow to me. I felt I had let down myself and my family – but above all the players and the club. Because at Aberdeen when I was shown the red card in the first half we were trying to clinch the title and the players had to get the result we needed with only ten men.

The fact that the players showed the courage, the determination and the ability to go on and get the one point required to take the championship helped ease my own dejection. But I was still aware of letting them down a little. . . . But it wasn't just being ordered off. Other things surrounding the incidents didn't help my feelings one little bit. Opposition players appeared to want to land me in trouble with the referees. They went out of their way to challenge the match officials almost every time I made a tackle.

It was so bad during the season that I spoke to the Players' Union boss Tony Higgins regarding the problem. Personally, I think it is wrong to try to get a fellow professional in trouble. It's not something I experienced in England or in Italy, and it saddened and disappointed me that it should happen so frequently in my home country of Scotland.

For a week or so I thought about my future, and immediately after the game at Pittodrie I was ready to quit playing and concentrate on management.

Gallacher: Yet, initially you felt that you could play for three more years when you signed. . . .

16

The power, the aggression, the determination of Rangers' skipper Terry Butcher see him win this ball in the air from a trio of Aberdeen players – David Robertson, Willie Miller and Davie Dodds – in a Premier League game at Ibrox. Butcher, says Souness, is a winner

Souness: Oh, yes, and that hasn't changed any. I feel fit and I still have an appetite for the game, but all these annoying distractions on the field depressed me. Still, I'm over that now. I'll play on and I look forward to being in the European Cup. That is the big one after all.

As regards your other questions earlier. It's hard to say whether it was harder or easier than I thought. Let's say it was demanding – but at the end of the day, rewarding. More rewarding than I could ever have believed when I took on the job a year earlier. To be honest I think winning the championship brought us in a little bit ahead of schedule. I didn't think that the players would be able to provide that kind of all-year-long consistency which title-winning teams have to show. But they did – and they proved me wrong. I honestly expected that we might win a cup – a short, sharp tournament was going to be more suited to the team we had.

The style which has made Souness such an influential player during his career, captured in this action shot

Then we won the Skol Cup, strengthened the team again, and plugged away in the League until suddenly there we were at the top.

But playing and managing is a demanding situation. Yet I am glad that I have done it. It brought me more satisfaction, winning the Premier League title, I mean, than winning any of the prizes I won with Liverpool. It meant more than any of the European Cups or First Division championships I picked up at Anfield. It was very, very special and to start off a new career with success is always a good thing to have happen to you. Obviously I just want to have it happen again. And *again*. . . .

The championship will always be the target for Rangers as long as I am manager. For me it is the best for any team. When you win the title then you are the best team in the country. You have proved it and no one can take that away from you. I felt we were the best team last season, and when we eventually won by six points it was gratifying for all of us at Ibrox.

Gallacher: You say the title is the number one prize, but you do have European ambitions do you not?

Souness: Of course we do – and very big European ambitions at that. I would love to do really well in Europe and to make this club

Hamilton's Gerry McCabe wins this time at Douglas Park as he edges the ball away from Ibrox boss Graeme Souness

talked about all over the Continent. When I came here to take the job I said that Rangers should be up there with clubs such as Real Madrid and I believe that. In fact I believe it even more now than I did when I arrived in Glasgow!

It's possible that we can do well. We were desperately close last season to having a very powerful run in the UEFA Cup. We got Borussia at the wrong time. Another month or two and we would have been ready for them. As it was we came close to knocking them out. We saw what Dundee United did, and I'm sure we could have marched on alongside them given a little bit of a break against the West Germans.

But the title is the supreme test for any team, and winning it is the passport to the European Cup. So you have to make that the priority in your thinking. As long as I remain manager that will be how this club and its players think at the start of every new season. They will see the championship flag as the major target.

Gallacher: You say there, just as you said earlier, 'as long as I remain manager'. Do you see yourself leaving the club?

Souness: That's not for me to say, really. The directors usually decide that, don't they. But if you are asking what I would like to do in the future I can tell you that I want to stay here as Rangers' manager for as long as the club wants me. I've moved around a little bit in my career, and now it's time to settle down and bring up my family. I'm with one of the greatest clubs in the world, I'm back home again and will be living with my family in Edinburgh from now on. Things have never looked better. I'll stay. There is no place else I would rather be as a club manager.

Gallacher: How about your international career? Is that over?

Souness: Last season I made the point to Andy Roxburgh, the Scotland team boss, that I had a lot to contend with. It was my first year as a manager and I was playing in a very competitive League as well. I had made a major commitment to Mr Holmes and to this club and I did not see my way to being away from the club for extended periods playing for Scotland. I'm sure that Andy understood the situation perfectly. It was a difficult time, and it would not have been the right thing for me to do. There was no way I wanted to divide my attentions in any way at all. I had to concentrate on my job at Rangers.

Gallacher: Did you miss the involvement with Scotland?

Souness: Yes, I suppose I did miss it. I'd been with the squad for a lengthy spell remember, covering three World Cups. But I didn't have a lot of time to miss it too much. After all I did have a lot on my plate.

Gallacher: How did you find the standard of play in the Premier League?

A double celebration early in the season when Terry Butcher joins his boss Graeme Souness after the pair had been voted 'Personality Player' and 'Manager of the Month' in the Scottish Brewers' awards. The Teddy Bear didn't win anything. . . .

Souness: I found the standard of the top teams, in particular, very high indeed. When you are playing Celtic or Aberdeen or Dundee United or one or two of the others then you know that you have been in a game. The lads who came up from England found that out very quickly. It is a very competitive League and it is a League where the game is played at a helluva pace all the time. But I wasn't surprised at the standard of play or the good individual players who play for the Premier League clubs. Remember I played with a lot of the lads in the Scotland teams down through the years. There were always players from the Premier League in the international set-up – and all of them would have been able to command a place in any of the top English teams.

I knew that it would be hard. I knew that it would be competitive. And, really, I welcomed that.
Gallacher: You like the game being highly competitive then?
Souness: I do and so do the players I signed. People like Terry Butcher and Graham Roberts like that edge on a match. They are

like myself basically, they are winners. I like winners. What we want to have at Ibrox is a whole team of winners, because it's only winners who lift trophies regularly and we won't settle for any less than regularly lifting championships and cups now that we have started.

Gallacher: I suppose that the Scottish Cup game against Hamilton was your only bad moment of last season at least as far as domestic games were concerned?

Souness: I don't know if it was the only bad one – there were one or two others. But it was certainly the worst.

It was one of the worst moments of my whole career in fact. I've never felt as low as I did that day. We were going well in the League by that time and there was a good feel about things. We had beaten Celtic on New Year's Day at Ibrox, and then I had felt there was a growing confidence about the team and about the individual players too.

But the one sure thing in this game is that it will kick you in the teeth. That's what happened to us that day. Two weeks earlier we had beaten Hamilton in front of a near sell-out crowd. And that day, the first round proper in the Cup, attracted just short of thirty-five thousand people to see a team at the bottom of the League, remember! Everyone expected us to win, but then that is always the time you are most likely to fall down. We fell down and it was not a pleasant experience.

As I pointed out earlier I thought we were better equipped as a cup team, able to handle a short sharp campaign rather than the marathon long haul of the title race. So it was vitally important for us to stay in the Cup and have a real go for it. Even though we were picking up League points and setting off on a charge for the championship, deep down I thought the Cup was our best bet for a second trophy. So, you can imagine how I felt when Adrian Sprott scored that goal against us. I have never, ever felt as low as I did that afternoon at Ibrox. It was a disaster for the fans, a disaster for the club and a disaster for the players. Luckily it didn't take us long to get over it as far as results were concerned . . . the next week we went to Tynecastle and won 5–2 there. But the scars from that day are still with me – and they will be there for a long, long time to come. I keep telling you I'm a winner and any defeat hurts, but that kind of defeat is the worst of all to take because it was a game we should have been able to win easily. We beat Hamilton in all four Premier League games, for example, but on Cup day we had to go and lose. It was humiliating and it hurt deeply.

Player-boss Souness and young midfielder Derek Ferguson both go for this high ball at the same time

Another of the big signings made by Souness from English football. Here is goalkeeper Chris Woods with his wife Sarah, five-year-old son Mark and two-year-old daughter Laura

Gallacher: The new signings you made in the close season have helped strengthen the squad again. Were they made specifically with Europe in mind?

Souness: Not at all. They were made to make sure that the squad is as powerful as we can make it. Someone like Avi Cohen, for example, has tremendous experience at all levels and he can play in one or two different positions. You always have to think along the same lines as Liverpool when it comes to a squad situation. You want eighteen or so players who are all capable of playing in the first team. That's the only way to maintain success in the game today.

Gallacher: How did you feel about the way the fans accepted the style of game you brought with you, something fairly clearly based on the pattern of play at Anfield?

Souness: I was happy with the way the supporters reacted. I think that some of the critics felt the Scottish fans wouldn't like a more patient build-up because that hadn't been the way of the Premier League. But it didn't take long for our supporters to realize what we were attempting to do.

They accepted it and they backed us. I couldn't have asked for any more from them. I mean, I've been around a bit in the game and I don't know of any supporters anywhere who are more dedicated to the club than the Rangers supporters are. They helped make the season for me and for the rest of the new players.

You think back to the way they turned up in huge numbers at Ibrox, to the way they backed us in the Skol Cup Final, to the way they travelled in their thousands to Aberdeen for that crucial League game. It took your breath away. And, even when we disappointed them, they still kept faith with us. After the Hamilton game they didn't turn their backs on us. They were there at Tynecastle the following week urging us on against Hearts. They helped get us back on the right road then. . . .

And in Moenchengladbach after we had drawn 0–0 in the second leg but still went out on goal difference they hid their disappointment and stayed on the terracings and cheered us. That meant a lot to every player who was there in that stadium. We felt we should have won that game, and the fans obviously agreed with us. Apart from that display of loyalty they didn't cause one little bit of bother. In fact they were praised by the West German police for their good behaviour. That meant a lot to the club as well in this difficult time for any British club going abroad.

Gallacher: Have they really been that important to you and the other signings you made?

Souness: Oh yes. There were times when I played for Scotland and the Hampden fans gave me a hard time, so it was good to arrive at Ibrox and find them right behind me. And I know that the English lads have been very grateful to all the supporters who have welcomed them. Honestly, they should all be picking up medals along with the players – that's how important I think they have been.

All I want is to give them even more success in the future, and to know that they will stay with the team through the odd disappointments we may have to come. All of us want to go on winning honours. For ourselves. For Rangers. And for the fans.

FINISHING OFF THE FINNS

If player-boss Graeme Souness had had any preferences as he led Rangers into Europe for the first time, then surely Ilves Tampere would have been high on his list of candidates.

But with that natural caution honed by his years at Anfield and the European experience he picked up there, Souness was not ready to say that. Instead he remembered playing another Finnish side in another European tournament when he was Liverpool's skipper. And he stressed how dangerous and how difficult that tie had been for a team with so much more experience in Europe than the Ibrox side he was re-modelling.

Rangers had plunged out of Europe in the first round of the UEFA Cup a year earlier to the little known Spaniards Real Osasuna from Pamplona. They wanted desperately to go further this time around. . . .

And no chances were being taken that they might be surprised by what appeared to be a fragile Finnish side in the first round. Spy trips were made, opposition was assessed and always Souness warned of the dangers which could lurk in the easiest of matches.

But what even his experience could not have told him was the ease with which Rangers won the first leg at Ibrox. And exactly how they did so.

Most of it was down to the chunky blond striker Robert Fleck whose career with Rangers seemed to be over at the start of the season. He had been left out of the first-team plans then and at one stage it looked as if the new regime were ready to let him go.

The twenty-one year old, though, had other ideas. He wanted to stay with the club and he aimed to impress Souness and assistant manager Walter Smith enough to want to keep him.

He started to do that in training, and in the reserve games where his form picked up and his pace began to be utilised properly. Then a few days before the tie with Tampere he started to do it in the first team as well. Not the most glamorous of games. In fact, in

The boss in European action. Rangers' player-boss Graeme Souness in action against the Finns in the UEFA Cup tie at Ibrox

one of the least glamorous of Premier League matches – against the part-timers of Clydebank.

But if the opposition was something less than impressive, Fleck's performance confirmed the growing view of the backroom staff that he was ready to make an impact in the first team. He scored a hat-trick that day in a powerfully solid Rangers win.

That earned him his place in Europe against the Finns – and he repaid the faith of his bosses by scoring a second hat-trick. The three goals inside a twenty-one-minute spell killed off any slight hopes that the Finns might have harboured of shutting up shop.

Earlier these plans had been affected in any case when their tough-guy defender Pekka Heino was ordered off by the Danish referee after only twenty minutes. Heino had set himself out to be

The hat-trick Robert Fleck scored against the Finnish team Ilves Tampere helped him into Scotland's Under-21 side. Here he is in scoring action for the international babes as he notches one of the four goals in the win over the Republic of Ireland

Tampere defender Petri Ojali is just too late to block this shot from a
determined-looking Graeme Souness

the hard man of the defensive strategy the Finns had worked out. At thirty-five he was their most experienced player and seemed convinced that by hard, harsh and often cruel tackling he would be able to stem the tide of attacks set up by the Scots.

The Danish referee had other thoughts. He booked Mikko Korhanen and then when that did not appear to be warning enough he sent off Heino for a vicious tackle on Ally McCoist.

Ten minutes later Fleck scored the opening goal. Winger Davie Cooper sent in one of the many free kicks Rangers were forcing and there was the giant figure of skipper Terry Butcher at the near post. He knocked the ball on and Fleck was there to finish things off. That killer instinct close in on goal brought the second of his three goals just on the half-time whistle. The overworked Tampere goalkeeper scrambled a shot clear and it was Fleck who pounced to snap the ball into the net.

In fifty-one minutes Davie Cooper showed all of his magic to set up the third. The huge 28,000 crowd rose to him as he weaved past a bewildered pack of Finnish defenders before laying on an easy scoring chance for the twenty-one-year-old striker.

Before the end Fleck's partner up front, Ally McCoist, added a fourth and Rangers appeared to be coasting into the second round.

But if the Rangers team went in to the Ibrox dressing rooms expecting to be praised by their new boss they were in for a shock. Souness who had gone off injured halfway through the second half was there to tell them, 'That was a sloppy performance and I want better than that in Europe. . . .'

His standards were set high from his years at Liverpool and the players were told what was expected from them in no uncertain terms.

But the biggest tongue lashing of all was still ahead of them, waiting in the damp and dreary textile town of Tampere. While warning after warning was being handed to the younger Ibrox players, injuries were piling up alarmingly. So that when the team travelled to face the second leg of the tie Cammy Fraser, Derek Ferguson and Ted McMinn were all left behind at Ibrox for treatment to injuries. Meanwhile player-boss Graeme Souness was also set to miss the match because of an injury which was troubling him.

Rangers, following the pre-match planning that Liverpool always used in Europe, jetted out twenty-four hours before the game not knowing what their line up would be.

Souness stressed: 'We don't want to come here simply protecting a lead. We want to come here and show a bit of skill. We have to be cautious and we have to be careful – but that shouldn't

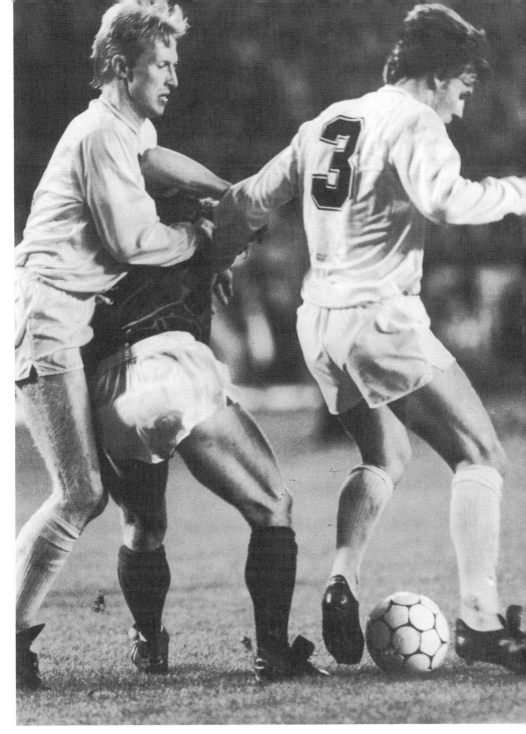

Here is one way to stop the opposition – two Finnish defenders tackled Robert Fleck in a most unusual way. This time they won, but Fleck had the last laugh with his hat-trick!

Eccentric winger Ted McMinn moves clear of a late challenge by
Tampere's English import Mike Bellfield in Rangers' four-goal Ibrox
victory

prevent us stringing together passes. We all know that anything
can happen in this game.'

And if the words from the manager were not enough, there was
added wisdom from skipper Terry Butcher who had been in the
Ipswich team which won the UEFA Cup five years earlier.
Butcher recalled one of the games they played then, against a
Greek side, Aris Salonika. At Portman Road they had hammered
them out of sight winning 5–1.

'It was different in the second leg over there,' he grimaced. 'At one stage they were three goals up on us and just another one would have put us out of the tournament on the away goals counting double rule.

'Then little Eric Gates scored for us and that was enough to take the pressure off and make sure that we would be in the next round. But it was a nerve wracking ninety minutes.'

Not that Butcher or Souness thought that Rangers would lose five goals to the Finns. Not in their worst nightmares could anyone see that happening. But they wanted to instil good European habits into the team and with four goals tucked away in the bank, this was as good a time as any to preach a little common sense to the players who lacked the know-how which can often help carry a team through in Europe.

And with the Finns adding their own views that maybe, just maybe, this time they could get revenge, the message to the players was being carved out in capital letters.

Unhappily the warnings were to be ignored!

One time Wimbledon player Mike Bellfield made it very plain that he and his Finnish team mates were out to make life uncomfortable for the Scots. Bellfield, who had been in soccer exile in Finland for six years, suspected there were flaws in the Rangers make-up that he and his part-time pals could exploit.

'Things went right for them in the first leg,' he maintained. 'We lost a player early in the game and then they picked up goals easily. We won't allow that to take place again. OK, not one of us honestly thinks that we can get through to the next round of this tournament, but believe me we want to go out with a bit of dignity left. If we can win this leg of the tie then it will give the team and the fans a lift. Because of the first game we have been in disgrace with the supporters here. We have to change that.'

Indeed only a couple of thousand turned up to see the clash – and the locals who stayed away missed a night of embarrassing defeat for the new-look Rangers. Their problems did not really begin until after half time, and they never reached the proportions of those which had haunted Terry Butcher since that Cup clash in Greece. But they did have Souness storming after the game that Rangers had 'played like a pub team'.

Ruled out of the tie himself he paced the track anxiously as he saw his players slump to their worst display since he took over as boss. Perhaps things might have been different if Ally McCoist had scored in the first half, when he broke clear of the Finnish defence and struck a shot against the post. It was the best scoring chance of the game until the referee from Czechoslovakia gave Tampere a penalty eight minutes into the second half. International striker Ari Hjelm went crashing down after a challenge from Dave McPherson. He recovered to take the kick and sent it confidently away from Chris Woods. Exactly twenty minutes later the Finns grabbed a second and Rangers' embarrassment was complete as the small groups of their own fans huddled unbelievingly around the ground. It had not seemed possible and while they recovered to play out the remaining time without any real worries the nagging doubts remained as to how this had happened.

As Souness had remarked: 'Anything can happen in this game. . . .' And as Terry Butcher pointed out, he had played in a game where his side had come close to losing a four goal lead. Similar stories abound in European football.

Sometimes upsets come because of refereeing decisions which go against a side. . . .

Sometimes they come because of injuries which have fallen between the two games and leave a team short of several key players. . . .

Sometimes they come when a team freezes in the kind of intimidating atmosphere which can be found in Milan's San Siro or Turin's Stadio Communale or Madrid's Bernebeu.

But none of these could explain this flop by Rangers. They did have a penalty given against them but the refereeing was not poor enough to knock the team out of its stride.

They were without players. The imposing figure of Souness himself was missing and so was the experience of Cammy Fraser. And even the usual stand in for the player-boss Derek Ferguson was out. Burly striker Colin West was in plaster. But Souness did not look there for excuses. After all, they were playing a team who were in the middle of the Finnish First Division. A team of part-timers who should never have been allowed to gain the initiative.

The players were told that. Bluntly. Savagely. Honestly. The display was not up to the standards demanded by the new regime. Better was asked for the next time.

In hindsight perhaps it was a good thing for Rangers to receive a jolt in a game which they had already won. That way it was brought home to them personally. Not in the cautionary tales of Souness and Butcher, or in the stories of what had happened to other clubs. They learned the lesson themselves and they managed to learn it when only their pride was hurt.

At the end of the day they were in the second round where they wanted to be. And when the draw was made forty-eight hours later they found themselves paired with Boavista of Portugal. No part-timers here – but a side hardened by year after year of European experience. This was going to be a test!

The shooting power which brought Robert Fleck goals with Rangers last season is shown here in a clash with Aberdeen

SEÑOR ALVES IS SILENCED IN PORTUGAL

Joao Alves made his reputation in Scotland as the black-gloved architect of Boavista when they faced Celtic, and of Portugal in international clashes with Scotland.

The gloves were his trademark when he first came to fame as a silky, skilful midfield player with the unfashionable side from Oporto. When he moved on to Benfica the gloves remained and so did the skills which made him celebrated around Europe. When he returned last season the gloves were off. He was back as the coach of Boavista, the home-town team where his career had started, and he was in charge of them in their UEFA Cup second-round tie against Rangers.

Only this was not the Alves people remembered. I could think back to the slim, quiet man who had graced so many games. But after the first-leg match at Ibrox when almost forty thousand people crowded into the stadium to see the clash, Alves had changed. He was transformed into a man spitting fury and promising revenge when the Scots travelled to Oporto to the second leg of the game.

The match had been marred by some tough tackling. It had also been spoiled to a large extent by the play acting and time wasting of the Portuguese. But that was not what concerned Alves on the night. His players were blameless – and Rangers would be made to suffer in the return!

Yet to the fans, all that happened was a throwback to the early years of European football when Continental teams came to Scotland and hurled themselves down at the slightest hint of a strong but fair challenge. They would resort to time wasting and intimidation of the referee as they tried to survive either for victory or until the second leg was played on their own ground.

Boavista were a powerful side, so much more experienced, skilful and impressive than the men from Finland who had lost to

A sample of the treatment Ted McMinn received in Europe – this was against the Portuguese side Boavista at Ibrox. And their coach complained!

Above: Down goes McMinn again, sent tumbling here by the Boavista defender Casaca as Rangers chased the lead they wanted to take to Portugal

Right: Youngster Iain Durrant moves forward on the ball as a Portuguese defender lies in wait for him

Rangers in the first round of the competition. This was the kind of hurdle you had to clear if you were to have any ambitions for European success. Rangers have always had these ambitions – Graeme Souness was now underlining them with a streak of thorough professionalism.

When he took over at Ibrox, Souness made it plain that he wanted a team which played in the Liverpool style. As the season progressed he converted the fans to the patient build-up and the more studied play which had brought his former club so much greatness. And, in Europe too, he dwelt heavily on the experience he had picked up in so many European campaigns with the Anfield club, as well as his playing experience with Sampdoria in Italy.

Throughout the build-up to the tie he emphasized how important the away leg could be. Away goals count double in European ties if the teams have drawn. That was never far away from the Souness thinking.

He insisted: 'This team beat Fiorentina of Italy in the last round of this competition. If ever we required a warning then that is surely one. Quite apart from that, the standard of play in the Portuguese First Division is high.

'We cannot go hell for leather looking for goals in this leg. We have to remain composed and we have to remember that it is sometimes easier to score goals away from home in Europe today.

'Our main priority is to stop them scoring here at Ibrox. That is a must. It is vital to this club and to our future plans that we can go through to the next round in Europe. It gives us tremendous revenue and it would allow us to move into the transfer market again to keep on strengthening the side. It's the way Liverpool worked for years and no one has been able to tell me that they were wrong.'

The problem for Souness, though, was that the team did lose that so important away goal after just half an hour. And then some ten minutes later with Rangers back level, the player-boss

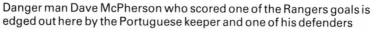

Danger man Dave McPherson who scored one of the Rangers goals is edged out here by the Portuguese keeper and one of his defenders

A hat-trick star from the first leg of the tournament Robert Fleck was obviously marked down as a player to watch. Here he is being marked by two of the Boavista men

mystified the huge crowd by dramatically running from the field to be substituted by the eccentric talents of Ted McMinn.

It was only after the game that he revealed, 'I felt my troublesome calf muscle injury start to go again. I didn't want to take any chances so I came off immediately. I've never been seriously troubled by injury but I knew that I couldn't go on.'

That, plus the loss of the goal was a serious blow to the Scots. They had gone behind when the Brazilian striker Nelson, one of the foreign players with Boavista, broke clear on the right.

He had been mentioned as the danger man of the Portuguese side by assistant manager Walter Smith after a spy trip – and how he confirmed that view. He went past full-back Stuart Munro and whipped the ball across goal for the striker Tonanho to score with a marvellous shot.

The crowd were stunned into astonished silence. This was not what they had come to see. But it was only three minutes before they could start to sing their team's praises once again, because that's how long it took the determined Rangers to wipe out the shock lead. A corner from Davie Cooper – so important so often for Rangers down through the years – deceived the Portuguese

The Boavista players celebrate after Toninho has given them the lead and Graeme Souness walks dejectedly away from goal with his head bowed – but Rangers had the last laugh with their win in Portugal!

defenders. The keeper missed it too and Dave McPherson roared in to snap a header into the net.

Then came the second shock when Souness went off but Rangers drew on all their resources to give the huge crowd a second goal a minute before half time. A raking, dangerous through ball from Terry Butcher released Ally McCoist. He beat off one challenge and then coolly hit a shot past Hubart and into goal for the Ibrox men to take the lead.

In a bad-tempered second half two of the Portuguese players were booked and the Swedish referee Bo Helen refused powerful claims for a penalty when McMinn was scythed down in the closing minutes. Instead, somehow, the referee awarded an indirect free kick.

That was forgotten though after the game when Alves appeared at the press conference, and began a savage attack on Rangers and their players. And also on the referee.

His major target was England star Terry Butcher and Alves insisted angrily that the Ibrox skipper should have been sent off after a first-half tackle. 'There were two tackles which should have given Butcher a red card,' he stormed. 'In Portugal the first one on its own would have had him back in the dressing room. But the second would certainly have had him sent off in any country. I do not understand why he stayed on the field.'

Butcher, of course, was not even cautioned for either of the incidents which so inflamed Alves.

Then, still with the gloves off and on the attack, he condemned the Rangers winner as 'very clearly offside. Only the referee and linesman did not see that.'

He then slammed Rangers for not allowing his players to train at Ibrox twenty-four hours before the game. 'We were sent to a small ground, a tiny ground fit only for growing potatoes,' he snarled. 'It was an insult and we shall report the whole thing to the European authorities.'

Then he added threateningly: 'That was a very violent game. My players feel angry and when Rangers come to our ground in two weeks' time that anger will remain. I am warning them now. We have been treated badly and we shall return that treatment.'

Later Rangers explained that no one could have trained at the ground because of the torrential rain which had been falling in Glasgow on the eve of the game. In fact they had trained at a nearby junior ground which Rangers use themselves on occasions. A puzzled Walter Smith said: 'All of this was explained to them. I cannot understand what they are on about.'

Neither in the end could the European Union. And the complaints from Señor Alves were dismissed.

But, of course, there was the problem of the second leg still looming. A problem made worse by the threats and also by the fact that Rangers had lost the away goal Souness had warned them of so often. And there was the worry over the player-manager himself. He had missed the Skol Cup Final at Hampden and in the intimidating atmosphere of the Bessa Stadium his very presence would be missed once more.

It was not the preparation that the Scots looked for as they flew out for that second-leg game. Added to that there came other threats from the Portuguese. Their English midfield man Phil Walker who had played with London clubs Millwall and Charlton, warned: 'Rangers had better not kid themselves. We want to win this tie and if that means being physical then that's what we will be. We won't be messing about. We thought we were badly dealt with at Ibrox and so we want a bit of revenge.'

The Boavista directors who had paid out a massive bonus of £1500 a man for the first-leg win over Fiorentina had now doubled this to beat Rangers. At the insistence of Alves the Portuguese players were set to pick up just short of £3000 each if they got to the third round.

Rangers might not have matched that bonus but in terms of personal ambition they too wanted to get to the third round and end a European jinx which had been haunting them.

Boavista, remember, needed only one goal to go through. One goal would give them their huge bonus. One goal would send Rangers toppling out of Europe. Only once in the fifteen previous years had Rangers managed to progress beyond the second round – Souness and the new breed of men running the team wanted that to change.

But even they did not realize just how dramatically it would be changed. Not by one of the experienced players they were probably relying on but by teenager Derek Ferguson, the kid who was in the team to take over the role normally played by Souness himself. On the eve of the match Ferguson had been named in the Scotland international squad by team manager Andy Roxburgh – and he celebrated that call up with the goal which pushed Rangers to victory. And into the third round of the UEFA Cup.

It was his new international team-mate Davie Cooper, named as a danger man by Boavista before the game, who set up the opening. With just less than twenty minutes left and with Rangers surviving Portuguese pressure, Cooper decided to take a hand in things. A deadly and decisive hand. He glided past three toiling Boavista defenders before nonchalantly laying the ball in front of the youngster. Ferguson responded to that little bit of magic by firing in a tremendous right-foot shot which raged into the net.

In the opening minutes his off-field mate Iain Durrant had almost given Rangers the goal they wanted so much. But, then, after half time it was the Portuguese who looked as if they would get the goal to decide the tie. Close-season signing Chris Woods proved his value with a world-class save from the Boavista striker with the famous name, Jose Augusto. That and an escape when Cammy Fraser cleared a try from Walker seemed to lift Rangers.

But while there were few on-field clashes, the hate campaign which had been directed against the Scots struck the bench after Ferguson scored. As Souness and his backroom staff celebrated on the track they were pelted by missiles from the crowd. And in that tense last spell of the game a mounted guard was placed around them as the fans hurled their hate. . . .

None of that mattered at the end, though. The theory which Souness had stuck to, that it was easier at times to score away from home in Europe, had come right for him.

Perhaps he had not expected it to come so right. And so soon. And in such a vital manner. But the goal meant that Rangers

It didn't take long for Derek Ferguson's clever midfield play to be recognized by his country. Here he is playing for the Under-21 team in their Ibrox victory over West Germany

would march on in Europe with another glamour tie before Christmas.

And even the hard-to-please Souness admitted: 'That was a pretty special result. Since playing the first leg you have to remember that we had a Skol Cup Final against Celtic and then, on Saturday past, another game against Celtic at Parkhead. It was a punishing programme and that's what makes this result particularly pleasing for me.'

Then he added: 'That save from Chris Woods was magnificent. It shows exactly why I went out to spend big money on him in the summer. It was a tremendous save at a very important time in the game for us. If that ball had gone in they would have been in front and had a boost. When he saved it the lift came our way.'

Now Rangers were drawn against Borussia Moenchengladbach, a team with a top European pedigree. The West German cracks were to be the barrier between Rangers and the place in the quarter-finals they coveted so much.

IBROX IS HOME FOR ME
says Graham Roberts

My first taste of the fabulous Rangers support came at Hampden last season when Rangers beat Celtic in the final of the Skol Cup. I wasn't playing. I wasn't even a Rangers player at the time – and I wouldn't be for another two months. But I was there as a member of the crowd, a huge Hampden crowd of 74,000 for the game which gave the club their first trophy under the gaffer, Graeme Souness. I was still a Spurs player, hoping for a move, but never dreaming that the move I would get would take me to Rangers to be a part of the brave new world being put together at Ibrox.

I'd come up to see the game with Richard Gough. He had almost joined Rangers in the summer, but when his club Dundee United refused to sell him to another Scottish club he ended up at White Hart Lane – and he persuaded me to travel north for the match. We were just like any of the other punters – a couple of drinks in Jim Baxter's pub and then off to Hampden and even then, just as part of the crowd, I sensed that Rangers were something special. Since I signed I have realized just how special the club is.

Not because we were able to win the League, though obviously that helped. But because of the whole stature of the side. I didn't have any doubts when Graeme Souness came in for me. I knew then that Rangers were a club I wanted to join and that they were a club who were going places in a big, big way. All I wanted to do was be a part of that success story. No one down south quite realized the revolution which was taking place in Glasgow. I did. I saw it at first hand on that Sunday afternoon in October when the Skol Cup was won. And I had watched as my old England team-mate Terry Butcher was persuaded by the boss to make the move north of the border – giving Spurs the elbow to do it, incidentally! And Chris Woods had also gone to Scotland reversing the trend which over the years had always seen Scottish players move south in big money deals.

I watched, thought about it, listened to Richard Gough when he came south telling me what was happening and then saw it for myself at Hampden. Becoming a part of all of that was out of this world.

One of the Englishmen who took the 'high road' to Scotland before
Graham Roberts – his old England team-mate Terry Butcher

I don't say that lightly, by the way. In my time with Spurs I had my share of good times. I was in the two teams which won the FA Cup in successive seasons in 1981 and 1982. Each time we won after replays, with Manchester City first of all and then with London rivals Queen's Park Rangers. Then, two years later, we won the UEFA Cup, and I scored one of the goals at White Hart Lane against the Belgian side Anderlecht in the second leg of the final. It went to penalties before we could clinch the trophy, and that was an amazing night. But it can't compare with the way I felt at Pittodrie on the second last day of the season when we won the Premier League Championship. Or even on the final day when, with the League won, the fans turned the match against St Mirren into a gigantic celebration party. We knew we had to win again for them that day and we did, and at the end we were able to relax for the first time in months and enjoy the celebrations ourselves.

We honestly felt that we were the best team in the country last season – and winning the League surely proved that. Especially when we won the title by a fairly sizeable margin at the end of the day. It was strange that while people looked for us cracking under the pressure it didn't happen. Maybe we didn't play as well as we had done in earlier matches, but we were able to keep on stringing results together. And as we did that it was Celtic, our closest challengers, who snapped. They lost games on the run in, and we didn't slip once after losing at Parkhead in the Old Firm derby game. I must say that was a disappointing result for us – and for me personally. It was my first game at Celtic Park and I wanted to win it in the same style as we had won the game against them at Ibrox on New Year's Day.

That was my first Old Firm game and it lived up to all that I had heard about these matches. I don't think anyone can possibly realize the tension, the atmosphere, the electricity which seems to flow from the crowd, unless they have taken part. I was always told that this was the greatest club game in the world and that no derby game anywhere else could match it. Well, I played in my share of London 'derbies' and they were competitive, and hard, and each team desperately wanted to win, but the Old Firm match is on its own. I don't think that anything can compare with it. And when you know you are playing in that type of match then you know that you are with a top team and in a top-class League.

I have never held the views of people in England who sometimes criticize the set-up in Scotland. Now that I have played here for a spell I have come to respect the quality of play in the League. The top teams are as good as any in the English First Division. I'm talking about teams such as ourselves, naturally, and Celtic,

48

Opposite: The so influential player-boss Graeme Souness, still showing his on-field style

Above left: Souness at Ibrox with the League Championship trophy

Above right: England international keeper Chris Woods yells instructions to his defenders in a Premier League game

Right: The emerging talent of Derek Ferguson is seen here as Graham Roberts watches admiringly in the background

Below: Striker Ally McCoist moves clear of a tackle from Hearts defender Brian Whittaker

Above: Blond striker Colin West is surrounded by Dundee United players . . . Ian Redford and Dave Bowman are the closest two

Right: Former Spurs man Graham Roberts, who settled in so happily at Ibrox

Below left: It's trouble for Jimmy Nicholl here as he loses out in this aerial fight

Below right: Iain Durrant moves in ahead of Dundee United's Dave Bowman

Above: The first sight of Souness in a Rangers jersey — in the pre-season clash with Spurs at White Hart Lane

Below left: England star Terry Butcher, who became the Rangers captain and a hero to the fans at the same time

Below right: Not a big buy, not an international star, but still a first-team regular last season — left back Stuart Munro

Davie Cooper causes panic in the Dundee United ranks as his World Cup
companion of the summer Eamonn Bannon tries to get in a tackle

The highest of the day! Defender Dave McPherson outjumps everyone
in a game against Hearts – the team he joined in a close season
transfer deal.

Aberdeen and Dundee United. Maybe even Hearts could force their way into that category. Any of these teams would be challenging in England just as they challenge up here north of the border. Certainly, in the games I played against them I felt that I could not be involved in any which would be more difficult down south. Even the supposedly lesser teams have the ability to make things hard for you. Possibly they lift their game against Rangers. The other lads have told me that this happens, and I can believe it. I found that some of the bottom teams could pose problems – and did pose problems for us. I know that most people in England, either in the game itself, or simply football fans, would look at a match against Falkirk or Clydebank or Hamilton and reckon it would be a walkover for Rangers. That's not the way it works out . . . .

Hamilton proved that against us at Ibrox in the Scottish Cup tie – the absolute low point of my first season with the club. When you count being ordered off against them in the League game which preceded the Cup tie by a couple of weeks you'll see that John Lambie's men were hardly my favourite team. And then you had Falkirk beating Celtic on the day we drew at Pittodrie and helping give us the title a week earlier than any of us had expected!

As I say, no one in the south would ever expect these results, but they happen. And the smaller teams have good players and good organization to back them. I think that playing for Rangers and Celtic brings its own special problems, of course. The other teams do want to beat you and every match you play in is like a Cup tie. There is atmosphere in all of them. At the small grounds you will have sell-out crowds – at home you get Ibrox packed almost every week. All of that adds to the pressures, but also adds to the whole situation. It's when you walk out at Ibrox and see these stands full and hear the crowd roar that it's brought home to you just how great the club is.

Though, I have to say that the expectation of the fans does make a heavy burden for the players to carry at times. For instance, when we were locked in that race with Celtic at the top of the table at the end of last season. You could sense on the park the nervousness in the crowd. And it was so understandable, because they hadn't seen their team win the title for nine long years. Sure, they had had cup wins to celebrate, but in the Premier League all they had known was disappointment after disappointment, defeat after defeat as they chased the prize which counts most of all. The gaffer and Walter Smith tried to ease the tension we felt ourselves. They refused to talk about the title publicly, refused to accept that it could be won until we were mathematically sure of staying in front until the end of the season. But it was difficult not to feel for

Opposite: World cup star Davie Cooper crosses on the run

Ibrox striker Ally McCoist is foiled by the Luxembourg keeper in a European Championship tie when the Rangers man was a Scotland substitute. Later in the season he was first choice – a promotion applauded by Graham Roberts!

the fans, not to get caught up in the nervy atmosphere they created. I'm sure that is why some of our own performances towards the end of the season showed a nervousness and uncertainty which had not been there when I arrived at the end of December.

Then, we were behind Celtic, well behind them and, with the Skol Cup already won, I reckon all the lads felt that we might get another cup win in the Scottish Cup. We were chasing the title, no way would anyone at Ibrox give up on that, but Celtic did have a commanding lead and all we could do was to try to chip away at that by winning our own games and looking for them to slip up. Then I think we were playing really well – that lapse against Hamilton apart.

In my first five games we picked up full points and didn't lose a single goal. We beat Dundee United in my debut match, then Celtic, went on to win at Motherwell when I grabbed the one goal of the game. Then we added wins over Clydebank and Hamilton. Unhappily I was sent off in the Hamilton game. But in that spell we scored twelve goals and didn't lose one, and collected ten valuable title points. Apart from own bad luck in being shown the red card in that Hamilton game it was a perfect start with a new team and hopes of the title rose. . . .

One of Graham's tips for the top, Derek Ferguson, seems to be winning
this challenge for the ball with Celtic's midfielder Paul McStay

A black moment for Roberts. Hamilton's Albert Craig is on the ground as Robert Fleck remonstrates with him and Roberts claims his innocence – but the iron-man defender was sent off

But it was not until that late spell, particularly after we lost to Celtic in the League game at Parkhead, that nervousness set in and our form suffered. We did manage to keep on winning, but sometimes we were not doing it with the style we had shown earlier in the season.

As well as the challenge of the Premier League the advantage of playing in Scotland is also that you have the opportunity to play in European football. I loved the games in Europe with Spurs – the time when we were able to beat Bayern Munich and Anderlecht in the season we won the UEFA Cup. Or the memorable games with Real Madrid the following season when they beat us by one goal in the quarter-final and then went on to win the trophy. And the time before that when Barcelona beat us in the semi-final of the Cup Winners' Cup – and they also went on to win the competition.

These are great memories, and I was just sorry that Rangers had gone out to Borussia Moenchengladbach a couple of weeks before my transfer went through. I would have loved to be involved again in Europe – and speaking to the lads after I arrived at the club I learned how unlucky they had been against the West Germans. If they had gone through that one then maybe we could have been celebrating a European win as well as the championship! It's certainly on our agenda for the future. Europe is a

Full-back Stuart Munro comes clear of this sliding tackle by Motherwell full-back Fraser Wishart. Munro impressed the one-time Spurs man

tremendous attraction for top players, and it's there that you can learn so much about the game. The experience the team picked up in the half-dozen UEFA Cup games will be a huge help to all of them, especially the younger players. I know that all of us want to bring a European trophy to Ibrox – preferably the European Cup! And, personally, I have the Scottish Cup as a priority target as long as I stay with the club. The one sure way of at least partially wiping out the memory of that shock defeat from Hamilton is to get to Hampden and to lift a winner's medal there. It won't make up for the dreadful feeling of that day, but it will help ease the pain a little. I'd like to do that and just get Hamilton out of my system. They were the only team who brought two blots into my first season with Rangers and both times it hurt.

I knew that I came north with a reputation for being a hard man. OK, I do play hard – but I'm not dirty. Sometimes the problem is that when you do pick up a name for being a 'dirty player' then that precedes you. Opposition fans look for trouble from you and opposition players often look for bother that isn't there. Referees, too, can be brainwashed by publicity and crowd reaction into thinking that you are out for trouble. All I want is a quiet life, and a chance to get on with my career.

It upset me that the Spurs boss David Pleat had a bit of a go when I left. After two hundred games for them, and the successes I mentioned, I didn't deserve that. Personally, I don't think that some of his remarks helped my cause in Scotland. I could have done without that kind of aggravation. All of that saddened me. I had been a good servant at White Hart Lane and if the new boss there didn't want me in the team then that was it – it happens and as a professional you accept it. It's never easy to live with the fact that you are out of the reckoning for the first team, but it happens all the time. You don't sit down and mope, you pick yourself up and get on with your career. The fact that my career is on an upward swing again is a bonus for me. If I had stayed at Spurs I would have won nothing last season. Coming to Ibrox I lifted a championship medal and qualified to play in the Continent's top competition, the European Cup. That can't be bad – and David Pleat can say what he likes! I had good days with Spurs and I would rather remember them than the problem times at the end just before I was sold to Rangers.

I reckon my future looks good now, better than it might have been if I'd stayed in London. The main thing is that I'm now a part of a very professional set-up. One which has gained success already and is anxious to taste that success again. I'm playing alongside top-class players – Chris Woods, Terry Butcher and Graeme Souness himself, I knew and admired. I think we all had a

Roberts is swamped by his new team-mates after scoring against
Motherwell in only his third game for the club

mutual respect for each other when we were in opposition. And
the way Chris had that record number of shut-outs last season
proved how effect a goalkeeper he is. Terry is just one of the best
centre-halves in Europe, and Graeme remains a world-class
midfield general.

The bonus I have had, though, is from the other good players in
the team. Players who are younger and players I didn't know of
before making the move to Ibrox. The two young lads who play in
midfield, Derek Ferguson and Iain Durrant, can go all the way in
the game. I have been very, very impressed with the way they have
played and the way they handled themselves in the important

Another youngster admired by Roberts – Iain Durrant who is being
challenged here by St Mirren's Under-21 international Ian Ferguson

games at the end of the season. They tired a little towards the end – but it was a long, difficult season for them and they showed enough to convince me that they have the quality which will make them top-class players in the years to come. They will both play for Scotland. I'm sure of that.

At left-back Stuart Munro, another lad I didn't know, played in almost every game and just kept gaining in confidence. He really did tremendously well, particularly when you remember that he had more than fifty competitive games to play last year.

Then the boss plucked an unknown out of English soccer in Jimmy Phillips from Bolton. Again he wasn't a player I knew anything about and yet, after his arrival he had several runs in the first team, coming up from the substitutes bench and he looked a really good player. Jimmy surprised me. A good footballer and the kind of player the modern game needs. He seems able to fit into the team in several different positions, runs well and I'm sure he is set to make an impact on the club and the game in general in Scotland. . . .

Up front Ally McCoist was someone I knew from his short spell with Sunderland in the English First Division. He has matured now and learned a lot, both from his spell in the south and over the last season under the guidance of the gaffer. Don't forget he scored *thirty-five* goals for the club!

In any league that is formidable and in a League as competiive as the one we play in week after week it is an amazing total. I was glad to see Ally getting his chance with Scotland at the end of the season. He deserved that opportunity, and sitting in the stand at Hampden – a spectator there again – I enjoyed seeing him battle it out with big Terry Butcher in the Scotland v. England clash. I'm just glad he didn't score in that one, but I was willing him to get a goal a few days later against the Brazilians. He didn't, but I felt he played well.

With the manager signing other top players in the summer I'm sure that we will be an even better side and the competition for places will be fierce. Obviously Graeme Souness learned a great deal from his time at Liverpool. At Anfield they believed in having a strong player pool which they could dip into if anyone was injured or if anyone's form dipped a little during the season. The boss, I'm sure, will be aiming for that kind of situation at Ibrox. In the long run it will only benefit the club – and, hopefully, bring us more and more trophies.

I came up here to be a winner again. I've started well and I'm not finished yet. There are more celebrations to come for these marvellous fans who made me so welcome when I arrived last Christmas.

MISERY IN MOENCHENGLADBACH

When the draw was made for the quarter-finals of the prestigious UEFA Cup tournament, Ibrox supremo Graeme Souness stressed that Borussia Moenchengladbach would prove tough opponents. Just how tough Souness could not have realized, but always the battle-hardened player-boss, veteran of countless European ties with Liverpool, emphasized that the West Germans would be as difficult a team as any left in the competition. He went on record that early as saying that he would rather have been drawn to meet Terry Venables' Barcelona – that Spanish side of stars who were to be beaten in the quarter-finals of the same competition by Dundee United.

Souness did not fear the big names of Barcelona, the strike force of Gary Lineker and Mark Hughes, the strong smattering of Spanish internationals who made the Nou Camp their home, as much as he did the lesser-known Germans.

The Rangers support had had an early warning of the power of West German club football. In a pre-season friendly Bayern Munich had come to Ibrox and beaten Rangers 2–0. The game then was taken on as part of the learning process which Souness and right-hand man Walter Smith wanted the younger players to go through. The West German champions had not come to Glasgow to entertain – they had come to win the challenge game. And they did so by employing the counter-attacking methods which their nation has almost patented down through the years. They showed patience and they showed cunning. They showed skill and they showed lethal finishing. As for Rangers, they showed the kind of naivety that Souness and Smith had feared would be the case. That 'innocence' in the face of the well-worked out Bayern tactics brought disappointment and defeat.

Now Souness hoped that his players would remember the lessons of the pre-season clash. Time and again he stressed that there could be no relaxation of concentration during the ninety minutes. A moment's lapse could prove crucial, he underlined in all his pre-match talking.

Sadly he was to be proved correct in that first leg at Ibrox.

Rangers' left-back Stuart Munro, one of the victims of Belgian referee Alex Ponnet's eccentric decisions. He was ordered off in the second leg against Borussia in West Germany

Possibly the biggest problem of all for Rangers was that Souness himself was still out of action with the calf muscle injury he had collected in the game against Boavista of Portugal. That had kept him out of the Skol Cup win over Celtic at Hampden, and here for the so important first leg of the clash with Borussia he was still confined to the side lines. His experience, his European know-how would have meant so much to the Rangers team on the night they were asked to take on what Souness insisted was their toughest task of the season so far.

At the plush Turnberry Hotel where they prepared for the third-round tie Souness confirmed: 'Borussia are the team I most wanted to avoid after we got through against the Portuguese. I said that before the draw was made and anyone who knows me recognizes just how highly I rate the West German game.

'Basically, the Germans play the game the way I would like to see us play. They have marvellous technique, great, great patience and they will use a counter-offensive game that is so effective – particularly when you are playing away from home in a European tie.

'The way they can sit back and soak up any punishment then break quickly into attack and be threatening your goal inside just a couple of moves is a worry for us. We fell for that kind of a game against Bayern. We lost concentration a couple of times that night and we paid for it. They scored twice and it proved to me then that we didn't have the know-how for top-class European football. We have been improving since then, but it's essential that we don't lose an away goal in this first leg tie. That is very, very important.

'I think that nowadays European football has changed around a great deal. Years ago teams had to build up a substantial home lead – then when away goals began to count for double in the event of a draw things altered. Teams can sometimes find it easier to score away from home. The last time I was in a Liverpool side which won the European Cup it was achieved by our perform-ances away from Anfield. We were good at scoring goals away from home and the Germans will be trying to play that way against us.

'If we have learned enough of a lesson from the pre-season game against Bayern we should be OK. But we will have had to take that lesson to heart.

'If we have not, then we could be in a little bit of trouble, because this is without any doubt the biggest test the team has taken on since I became manager.

'It has to be a top-quality performance because the tie might be decided in the first leg here. If it is going to go in our favour then we cannot let them get a goal!'

The Germans, bossed by Jupp Heynckes, once a striker with them and with the German national side, had worries of their own as they jetted into Glasgow twenty-four hours before the game. Their first-choice goalkeeper was injured, their Norwegian num-ber two was off form and twenty-two-year-old Uwe Kamps was being drafted into the side. As he arrived in Glasgow Kamps admitted: 'This will be the biggest ordeal of my life. I don't like the British style of play and I have had very little experience of handling that kind of football.'

And a grim Heynckes added: 'We have our first keeper injured, and Erik Thorstvedt, whom we brought from Norway, cannot be risked in a game as important as this one is for us. He does not have the nerve for a European game where the play could become physical and where the Scots may play a lot of high balls. This is a worry for Kamps too – but he must play. We have no other choice.'

Knowing of the Borussia concern about Kamps and his worries

He's playing for Scotland here, against Bulgaria in a European
Championship game – but the treatment was the same in the Boekelberg
Stadium in Moenchengladbach for Rangers' winger Davie Cooper. But
while he was the target for wild tackling in two legs, it was Cooper who
was ordered off in the closing minutes of the match

over cross balls Souness began to toy with the idea of bringing back the burly Colin West, the striker bought from Watford in the summer.

The blond West had been out for three months after a nasty knee injury sustained in the game against East Fife in the Skol Cup. After an operation and a period of recuperation at a special injury treatment centre in England, West was fit again. It would be a gamble, but one Souness was ready to accept if he felt that the game could be won through West's power in the air.

In the end Souness was not to use that gambler's throw until the second half of the game, as forty-four thousand fans willed the Scots to a victory they could not achieve. Not because of any lack of effort. Not because of failure to score themselves. Not because

Orders from the boss. It was the influence of Souness on the team which Borussia coach Jupp Heynckes feared most of all in the second leg

they were unable to pierce the tough no-nonsense, fierce-tackling Borussia defence. Simply because the players forgot the warnings they had heard in the days spent at Turnberry. One moment's lapse of concentration allowed the man who had been marked down as the West German danger man, international midfielder Uwe Rahn, to strike.

Souness had warned constantly of the counter-attacking strengths of the Germans and stressed the need for 100 per cent concentration for the entire ninety minutes. Walter Smith, who had seen the Borussia side in action, returned to warn the players of the menacing runs made by Uwe Rahn from the midfield.

On the night, in less than a minute of madness, Rangers forgot all the warnings. It came at a crucial time in the game – just minutes before the interval with the Ibrox side leading by a goal from Iain Durrant. The speedy full-back Andre Winkhold broke clear of Stuart Munro out on the left side of Rangers' defence. He outpaced the Ibrox defender and then slung a cross into the middle. It eluded Chris Woods, and with no one there to pick up Rahn the blond German star came in to finish the move off with a header from almost on the goal-line. It was the classic sucker punch, and Rangers reeled into the dressing room at half-time knowing they had blundered badly.

Yet, until then, things had gone well. Indeed they could hardly have asked for a better start to the match. Their own midfield scoring expert Iain Durrant broke clear after Davie Cooper and Munro had worked an opening in the grim barrier of defenders erected by the Borussia team around their penalty box. The youngster raced onto the ball, moved into the box and as one of the Germans lunged into a flying tackle to stop him, calmly struck the ball beyond the nervous Kamps and into the net. It was the breakthrough Rangers had wanted, and as the game wore on it seemed that more goals would come.

The Germans showed discipline and organization and a capacity for ruthless tackling against Cooper and the eccentric Ted McMinn. But they showed little of the attacking qualities Souness had worried over in the early stages.

Ally McCoist might have scored a second, and Kamps made hurried but effective saves from Terry Butcher and Durrant as the Scots controlled the match. Then came that goal, the first time the Germans had tried to attack, the first time Chris Woods had been asked to make a save, the first time Rangers had been in any danger.

It was enough, however, to give the Germans the away goal they wanted. And needed! For no matter the Rangers efforts after half-time, they could not find the killer touch which had been there so early in the game when Durrant had struck for that opening goal.

Giant skipper Terry Butcher spent almost as much time in the Borussia penalty box as in his own. He was up for all the free kicks and corners that Rangers won time and again as they pushed into a non-stop attack trying to find the vulnerable chink in the massed German defence. Colin West arrived to join the fray twenty-five minutes from the end, but while chances did arrive the Germans were able to deal with them. And the longer the game wore on the more Kamps seemed to increase in confidence. At the death the young keeper saved from McCoist and McMinn as the pressure built around his goal.

He held out. His team-mates defended ruthlessly in front of him, and so the game ended in a 1–1 draw which gave Borussia a vital edge for the second leg in their own Boekelberg Stadium. With that precious away goal counting double Borussia were in command of the tie – if the score remained the same they went through. Rangers had to head for West Germany looking for at least one goal to carry them into the next money-spinning round of Europe.

Disappointed though he was, Souness immediately began to plan for the future – even beyond the next clash with Borussia. He started negotiations with Spurs for their experienced English international defender. It was to be a month before he landed his man – but recognizing the defensive problems which had still plagued them in Europe, Souness made his moves straightaway. He wanted more experience in the back four and he wanted a hardness there, too. The kind of hardness which Borussia had shown and which Roberts would be able to provide.

Before that deal could be completed, of course, Rangers had the second leg of their tie in West Germany and the priority for that was for Graeme Souness to be fit himself. He set that target, and with typical determination trained and fought for fitness so that he could be on the field to help his team in what was going to be a test of nerve as well as a test of skill and experience.

I felt that if Souness had been present on the field in the first leg then Rangers would have won. Most people would accept that view, and clearly if they were going to worry Borussia in the second game then a Souness comeback would aid the Scots cause.

That is why on a quiet Sunday morning, three days before the second-leg clash, Souness went to Ibrox and pushed himself through a punishing training session. Twenty-four hours earlier Rangers had stuttered to a draw at Easter Road against Hibs and picked up still more injuries. The situation was critical, and Souness knew it.

Young midfielder Iain Durrant who scored Rangers' goal in the first leg of the UEFA Cup third-round tie against Borussia Moenchengladbach at Ibrox

That is why he was at Ibrox. That morning he kicked a ball for the first time in seven weeks. He ran freely, felt himself moving without any discomfort and told me: 'I do need the feel of match conditions, but other than that I feel really good. The problem is maybe coming back too quickly. This game is vital for us – but so is the rest of the season.

'It would be foolish to take too much of a chance and then find myself sidelined again when we have important Premier League games coming up. All that has to be taken into consideration.'

Yet that day, the way Souness spoke convinced me that he was ready to take the chance. The next morning he came through the practice game and Borussia coach Jupp Heynckes listened to the news that he might return and admitted this would be a problem to his team. 'I think that we recognize how influential a player like Souness is,' said Heynckes. 'His presence on the field will help to lift Rangers. It is not something we expected and not something that we wanted.

'As well as that, Souness will be able to keep Uwe Rahn quiet. We count on him to score goals for us, and this will limit his chances. He will not have the same chances as he would have without Souness in that area.'

While the German fretted and worried, Souness allowed them no clues. He played his cards close to his chest until the last possible moment. It was only when the teams had to be named before the kick-off that Heynckes, learned that Souness would play. Until then he had veered between planning for the game on the basis that Souness would play – and then changing things around guessing that the man who had learned so much about European games in his years at Anfield was bluffing. Even on the morning of the game Souness was saying: 'I could go out there and have a nightmare. It's not an easy decision for me to make. . .' And as he told the Germans that, Heynckes made one plan after another, trying frantically to find out whether the Scot was bluffing in an attempt to unsettle the Borussia thinking.

He wasn't bluffing – but he did upset their pre-match planning and gave Rangers an edge as they went into the game.

Indeed, Souness went on to dominate the game. The absence didn't affect him. The seven weeks spent idle had not rusted the skills which had always been so superbly honed to European football. This was the stage he liked, and how he strutted across it displaying a style and arrogance that the West Germans could not match.

It was the kind of night Souness enjoyed, a night where he could revel in the big-match atmosphere of Europe, re-kindling memories of his days at Anfield. Heynckes had worried before the game –

Ted McMinn was used to punishment before he left Rangers. He was a target for the West Germans of Borussia, and here he is on the receiving end of a hand-off from Celtic's Peter Grant

he saw in the early stages that he had been right to concern himself over Souness. And the longer the game wore on the more evident it became that if the Ibrox player boss had been fit to play in the first leg, then Rangers would have been heading for the quarter-finals of the tournament.

The West Germans, in contrast to the confidence shown by Souness, were edgy and uncertain. They knew that they were in a winning position, and knew also to lose a goal to Rangers could be fatal. So while Souness struck the ball about and Rangers attacked, the Borussia men gathered themselves around their own penalty area, only moving forward with caution and only when they felt they were not allowing themselves to be vulnerable.

For that reason Rangers dominated the first half with Souness bossing the show and with Chris Woods taking up the role he filled so frequently in domestic games, as a spectator. It was into the second half before the blond Englishman was asked to make a save. He did so magnificently, showing the concentration and the style which had made him the first signing under the Souness regime. Before then Rangers had looked capable of winning the game – and therefore the tie.

After eight minutes play striker Ally McCoist smacked a long-range shot against the bar. Then just before half-time it was McCoist again who was desperately close to getting the goal the Scots needed. Then Terry Butcher had a header drift wide and saw strong claims for a penalty turned away by the eccentric and fussy Belgian referee Alex Ponnet.

Ponnet also allowed the West Germans freedom to scythe down Davie Cooper and Ted McMinn when these two showed the strong running and clever dribbling which had upset Borussia in the first leg. There was little protection offered, and as the Ibrox pair were hammered time after time Rangers began to lose some of their composure.

The longer the game wore on, the more pronounced were the problems caused by Ponnet. Until, finally, the referee over-reacted dreadfully, and Rangers had two players sent off. The first victim was Stuart Munro. The young left-back clashed with midfielder Andre Winkhold. The German aimed a kick at the Rangers player who had won the tackle. Munro retaliated – and it was Munro who went off, sixteen minutes from the end.

Then with only three minutes to go Ponnet sent off Davie Cooper when the World Cup winger complained to him after being fouled yet again by one of the German defenders. At first the Belgian official showed Cooper the yellow card – forgetting that he had booked the Rangers player in the first half at the same time as he had booked Uwe Rahn. Cooper ran to take up position for the free kick which had been given to Rangers when Ponnet realized his mistake. He then called Cooper back, and this time showed the player the red card and ordered him from the field.

It was an amazing error, and it angered the already furious Rangers players. When the whistle went at the end, skipper Butcher had to be restrained by Souness and coach Pete McCloy as he made for the referee and the linesmen. Eventually, the giant centre-half led the players to the Rangers end of the ground where

Goalkeeper Chris Woods shouts instructions, but the shouts were not enough against Borussia when the defence blundered to allow Uwe Rahn in to score

they saluted the supporters. Butcher, still in tears, recognized the boost the fans had given the team, and the players recognized that but for a lapse at Ibrox they could have been marching into the last eight of the prestigious tournament.

Butcher himself admitted on the flight back to Glasgow: 'I felt bitterly disappointed at what happened. We had put so much into the game and somehow we didn't get the reward we deserved. We should have won – the Germans knew that as well as we did. On the field during the game you could sense how apprehensive they were. They thought that because they had drawn at Ibrox they would win easily in front of their own fans. Well, we showed them that wasn't going to be the case. It hurts that we are not in the quarter-finals because we are a better team than them. . . .'

It was hard to disagree with that view of the match. Rangers, boosted by the Souness comeback, had looked organized and efficient. They had also played with European know-how which had been missing from the first leg. Souness had helped provide that extra ingredient – and he was as deeply disappointed as his captain at the result. He told me: 'I won't discipline the players who were ordered off – though the normal procedure at Ibrox would be that they would be dealt with by the club. Not this time!

'I know exactly how they felt, and I don't blame them for what happened. Terry Butcher was very, very upset at the end of the game. I felt that showed how much the big fellow feels for this club. We all felt bad because we were a better team than them over the two games. We should have been going on in the competition, and that would have been important both for us and for the fans.

'We want to be involved in Europe at the highest level for as long as possible. It's where the club deserves to be. . .'

Souness had felt that, perhaps, the side had too little experience for a serious assault on one of the European trophies. Probably, looking back to the sucker goal they lost at Ibrox, he was right. But on that cold December night in the Boekelberg Stadium his players came very close to proving him wrong. But for poor refereeing in both legs when their forwards were given little or no protection, Rangers might well have gone on just as Dundee

Striker Ally McCoist. He struck the bar early in the second leg of the game in West Germany

Skipper Terry Butcher, in tears at the end of the second-leg game when Rangers' European dreams died on the away goals rule!

United did in the same competition.

As for Alex Ponnet, while UEFA accepted his report and Cooper and Munro were punished, the Belgian FA eventually downgraded him in domestic football after poor reports from clubs in his own country.

That decision surprised no one at Ibrox!

WE'RE AHEAD OF
SCHEDULE says Walter Smith

When Walter Smith returned from Mexico where he had been number two to Scotland manager Alex Ferguson he sat down with another veteran of that World Cup campaign to plan for Rangers' future. Smith had moved from Dundee United to join Graeme Souness in a management team which would eventually take two of the three domestic trophies in Scotland. Yet, back in that summer when the planning talks were going on neither of the Ibrox pair believed that they would be able to win the trophy in their first year.

Smith admits that now, stressing: 'We are ahead of the schedule we had pencilled in for ourselves. Obviously we wanted to win the championship – that is the prize you always want above any other. Equally, it's the hardest of them all to win – and when we moved in at Ibrox, Rangers had not taken the title for nine years.

'What we hoped for was being able to take one or other of the two cups, either the Scottish Cup or the Skol Cup and mount a really serious challenge in the League. After all, the season before we had only just managed to scrape into Europe. We knew that was not what was expected of Rangers and we knew it had to improve. What we didn't think possible was that we could make such an improvement in our first season in charge. That was a bonus for us. And for everyone connected with the club.'

But, apart from the League success, and the Skol Cup victory, Smith has enjoyed more than anything else being part of the Rangers revolution. After years as right-hand man to Jim McLean at Dundee United, the man who now assists Souness has watched the transformation of the game in Scotland. He grins and admits: 'If anyone had told me just how much would be achieved by the club in such a short time I would never have believed them. I knew that I was coming into a big, big job with a big, big club. Even I didn't realize how big it was all going to be.

'I don't know anyone who could have done what Graeme has done here at Ibrox. He wasn't limited in any way when he came back from Italy. By that, I mean his horizons weren't set by the confines of Scottish football. He had played all his football away

72

Another of the Souness-inspired signings – skipper Terry Butcher wins
this ball in the air in a pre-season challenge against Bayern Munich. Colin
West looks on

from Scotland. He knew more of that great wide world outside our own boundaries – and when we couldn't get players at home then he looked elsewhere.

'That's the reason we went after Terry Butcher and Chris Woods, and I'm convinced that without Graeme there himself Rangers would not have been able to sign either of these two players. He had the kind of stature that they could admire. They had played against him when he was at Liverpool, and also when he was captaining Scotland. As well as that they knew his reputation inside the game and the very fact that he had decided to play the rest of his career in the Premier League with Rangers must have impressed them.

'The priorities were right too. If you are going to be successful then you must sort out the defensive side of things first of all. When we had Terry and Chris and then were able to add Graham Roberts we knew that we were solid in that vital area. At the end of the League programme we had lost fewer goals than any other side in the top division. Aberdeen were closest and Dundee United came after them, but neither of them came anywhere close to our goals for total. Only Celtic were able to do better than us there – but defensively they weren't able to match us at all. That's where we won the flag.'

Smith, of course, had been over the Premier League title-winning course before. When he was at Tannadice, Dundee United became champions and then went on to reach the semi-finals of the European Cup before losing to Roma. But he reckons it was harder for Rangers last year than it had been for United in his time there. He points out: 'I know how teams lift themselves to play Rangers. Remember, I had a lot of years seeing this from the other side. There's no doubt about that. When Dundee United went to Clydebank or places like that they didn't get the opposition fired up to meet them. They had other problems to overcome – the lack of atmosphere, for example, because there would only be a couple of thousand people maybe. But sometimes with Rangers the atmosphere lifts the other teams as well.

'Even when they come to Ibrox they can get inspiration from the size of the crowds we get there.

'And last year, of course, was that little bit more difficult because Rangers had not won the flag for so long and the fans were desperate to see us doing it. That got to the players, especially when we were in a winning position. Once we had got to the stage where we could still lose, the pressure was more intense than I'd ever known it at Tannadice in the year we were champions there. The public at large think it's just another trophy for Rangers, but it wasn't like that at all. Davie Cooper was the one player left at the

74

The man himself, Graeme Souness, has Hamilton player John Pelosi
going the wrong way here in a game at Douglas Park

Assistant manager Walter Smith has enjoyed the partnership with
player-boss Souness

club who knew what it was like to win the Premier League. And,
apart from him, only Graeme himself had won a title anywhere
else.

'That's why we had to try to cut down on all the talk from the
press and from the fans that we were going to win the championship. We didn't want that kind of talk. We just wanted to try
to keep things as low key as possible until we were really in the
position of having clinched things. It was difficult because once we
got to the top of the League the fans began to prepare for a title
win. That was hard for us to handle, and it was hard for the
players to handle as well. They did become edgy and a little bit

apprehensive, almost as if they were looking over their shoulders to see if Celtic were going to catch us up.

'On the run in we didn't play nearly as well as we had done earlier in the season, but we had to show a lot of determination too when it came to these last games. And we had to show some real grit as Celtic looked to place us under more pressure. Eventually, though, we did win and that was only what the players deserved after the season they put in. . . .'

But while that pressure built up slowly and surely, Smith was involved in other areas too. Souness and he were both aware of a troubling gap which existed in the young players who were being groomed for the first team. The emergence of Iain Durrant and Derek Ferguson as fully-fledged first-team men was another of the season's bonuses. So was the form and maturity shown by reserves Scott Nisbet and Dave McFarlane – but other players had to be

One of the bonuses for the Ibrox management team – Derek Ferguson. Here the young midfield man holds two awards as 'Young Player of the Month' and 'Personality Player of the Month' – a confirmation of his talents

found to bridge the gap between them and the much younger players. To do that the management team decided that big buys were not going to be the only important signings made by the club. Other lesser-known players had to be bought. Younger players who could be developed in the second team, and who could be ready long before the crop of youngsters for promotion to the League side.

Striker Neil Woods was bought from Doncaster for £100,000. He had been chased by Dundee United, as well, also hunting for players in the south. Midfield man Davie Kirkwood came from East Fife, and the youth international player had been watched by Manchester United and Liverpool. Then utility man Jimmy Phillips arrived from Bolton, and forced his way quickly into the first-team pool. Before the season ended he had played several times for the first team, always coming on as a substitute. But these were the players who were insurance for the future. . . .

Explains Smith: 'You are not in the position at Rangers where you can wait for players coming through from a youth policy, especially when you consider that any youth policy started by Graeme and myself won't show signs of bearing fruit for several years. With lesser clubs you can wait because the pressures of getting success are not nearly as great. But here at Ibrox people demand success from the team – and we have to react to that situation. There is no doubt that in the future we want to be producing our own players, youngsters who are brought up through the ranks. That takes time. Therefore we have to buy players just now, not only the top players for the first team but younger players who can develop in the reserves. Then, they can also be on hand as first-team pool players.

'That's why we have invested in people like Dave Kirkwood, Jimmy Phillips and Neil Woods, because while we were happy enough with the likes of Scott Nisbet and Dave McFarlane when they came into the side we also recognized the need for a stronger reserve set-up. It's essential to have a powerful player pool, to have cover for players who may go out through injury at important stages of the season. But we have not lost sight of the youth policy – it's just that we need time to see any fruits of success there for the hard work which is being done just now.

'We brought Gordon Neely here from Hibs to look after that side of things. He had been with me at Dundee United and I knew the players he had brought to Tannadice. Already we have set up training nights all over the country so that players get the chance to come along and work out under proper supervision. There were some areas where we felt the potential for signing young players had been neglected, and so we are working to build up a Rangers

Ferguson's midfield mate Iain Durrant – another of the youngsters
praised by Smith – challenged by Celtic's Paul McStay

presence all across Scotland. We want to try to ensure that we can get the best young players and then bring them along properly until they can be called up as full-time professionals. I saw the benefits of a well-operated youth policy when I was at Tannadice. We have to have that kind of approach here at Ibrox – and we have done a lot of important work over the past season. The entire scouting system has been re-organized and we will be in the market – and hopefully at the front of the queue – for the outstanding youngsters who might be available.

'I would doubt if anyone can match the set-up we have at Ibrox, but our job has been to get that message across to boys and parents. We made progress last season and we'll keep making progress.'

As well as the offer to make their career in soccer, youngsters wanted by the Ibrox club also get another opportunity – to carve themselves a career outside the game. The John Lawrence organization are ready to offer young players the chance of an apprenticeship within the group. As Smith stresses: 'We realize how important it is for any young lad leaving school to have a job available. And it would be wrong to ask them here as a player and then, if they didn't make it, suddenly leave them high and dry – particularly the way unemployment is these days. So we have a close liaison with Ian Elgy from the Lawrence group of companies. He advises the lads on alternative careers, and it is a little something extra that we can offer anyone who wants to come to the club.

'It can ease the minds of parents too, who might not see football as the best career possible for their sons. It has been good for us and good for the youngsters. We feel it's important for them to have some kind of back up away from the game.'

That, plus the new glamour surrounding Rangers, will give the Ibrox side the edge over many of their competitors. Smith knows from his years at Tannadice how many players Dundee United were able to sign under the noses of bigger clubs such as Rangers. That is something he has to combat, and he is working non-stop on ways of stopping the best players from escaping the Ibrox scouting net.

The work behind the scenes isn't often highlighted, particularly in a high-profile club such as Rangers. But the development of young players, the rearing of their own stars has often been neglected at Rangers. Today, even with the star signings, with the millions of pounds being spent, the smallest detail regarding the scouting set-up and the coaching and organization for the young players is attended to. That is seen as being just as important as looking after the big names.

80

Scott Nisbet, who impressed Smith and Souness during the season, challenges for a high ball in Scotland's Under-19 international with West Germany

Another of the Anglo imports – Graham Roberts comes in to win this ball
from St Mirren striker Paul Chalmers

For it's with the youth policy that the future of the club lies. Perhaps Rangers will never be able to boast a team of home-grown players. The special circumstances which surround the club, the demands made for constant, unfailing success, make it difficult for that to happen. Top players will always be bought because fans want to see them and top players want to be where there is success. Walter Smith knows this, and that's why as well as covering schoolboy games in Scotland he and Graeme Souness also spent many nights in England searching for fresh talent there.

The partnership put together by chairman David Holmes worked perfectly during the title winning season and also plotted well for the future. Smith added his unrivalled knowledge of the Premier League to the knowledge Souness picked up in his times with Liverpool and Sampdoria. And Smith smiles: 'The partnership which I formed with Graeme has been great for me. I have enjoyed it and it has been another part of the learning process for me.

'I worked a long time with Jim McLean at Tannadice and we had a close partnership, and I worked with Alex Ferguson at the World Cup and before that in the Scottish international set-up. They were the best managers to work with in the country, and now I am working with Graeme and it's different once again.

'I don't want to compare them at all because each one had his own way of working and that was always dictated by the circumstances of the club, or with Fergie the international situation. But Graeme has brought all the little things he learned with Liverpool into play since coming here, and I'm convinced after just one year that he is going to be a great manager. He has proved himself in his first season, and I don't see it stopping there. He has all the attributes of a top manager, and he wants to succeed in the job. I reckon he wants to make just as big a mark as a manager as he made as a player.

'He has been one of the most influential players of his generation at club and at international level. Even now I marvel at some of the things he does on the field. For my money he is still one of the best midfield men in Europe! All that and managing a successful team too. As a first season together I don't think either of us could have asked for anything better. But we want more success for the club. And we also want to make certain that we have a crop of young players ready to come through when we need them. You have to have that kind of back-up. Winning championships and cups is vitally important at Ibrox, but nothing can be neglected. Things have to be right from the top to the bottom and we're getting there.'

HOW THE TROPHIES WERE WON

The new-look Rangers had been given a taste of trophy-winning under the Souness management at the end of the previous season. . . . Then they had beaten Celtic in the Glasgow Cup Final, and that win was an omen their fans had hoped for. As the Ibrox team chased the important honours in the season ahead, this was to be the winning way, the Souness way!

And then it appeared that the Rangers support had been brought crashing back to earth after just one game in the Premier League. For in that opener to the new season on 9 August at Easter Road everything went hideously wrong. 'SOUNESS OFF' screamed the headlines that weekend as the Ibrox player-boss was sent off for a tackle on Hibs' George McCluskey. And, that apart, Rangers lost 2–1 with only a goal from Ally McCoist allowing some little consolation. It was a nightmare beginning, and Souness and his players knew it as well as every fan. . . . But Souness also knew that there had to be a fight back, that the League ran for forty-four games and disappointments had to be set aside if a team was going to win the title.

Two weeks later after a masterly performance for the first hour, Rangers lost again. This time they were at home to Dundee United, and after outplaying them for most of the match they crashed to a 3–2 defeat in front of a capacity crowd – the first of so many such crowds at Ibrox last season.

These two defeats were eased by wins over Falkirk and Hamilton, but it was not until the end of the month that the Rangers fans saw what they wanted – victory over Celtic! The suspended Souness missed the game and agonized at every move in the dug out. Youngster Iain Durrant, so often a vital goal-scorer, grabbed the one goal of the game and Rangers' fans felt their dreams could still have a happy ending. . . .

But the early glory came in the Skol Cup and not in the championship race. And it came with its share of hiccups too! Particularly in the second-round game at Methil against East Fife. For even there, again without Souness, it looked as if the glory the fans wanted so desperately would never materialize. On

84

The first trophy of the new Souness era! The Rangers team celebrate at Hampden with the Skol Cup and the League Cup

the Bayview pitch that the star Anglos had never heard of the Ibrox giants were taken to a penalty shoot-out.

A week earlier, with the player-manager scoring his first goal for the club, they had beaten Stenhousemuir 4–1 at Brockville. Then it was off to Methil, and as skipper Terry Butcher remarked later: 'I didn't know where the ground was. It had been difficult even recognizing where the Brockville pitch was when we played Stenhousemuir – but Bayview was really difficult.

'But I don't think after the game that I'll ever foget where it is. . . .'

Nor will striker Colin West, who had been the first of the Souness signings from England. Early in the game he was injured, stretchered off and it was to be three long months before he made another first-team appearance. West damaged knee ligaments, and it was only after months of treatment including a stint at the special FA rehabilitation centre in England that the burly man who had come north from Watford was ready to play again.

Anyhow, that game went to penalties and Rangers won 5–4 on aggregate to qualify for the last eight and a clash at Ibrox with Dundee. It was another difficult game – and around 34,000 fans at

Ibrox saw it go into extra time before Rangers eventually won by 3–1.

Then it was the semi-final, and a clash with the other Dundee team, the Tannadice-based United. At Hampden they won 2–1 thanks to goals from McCoist and the gangling eccentric Ted McMinn who was ultimately to move on to Seville and team up with his old Ibrox boss Jock Wallace.

Suddenly, the season which had started so gloomily had come alight. A League win over Aberdeen when Souness scored a spectacular goal in front of another sell-out crowd confirmed the growing belief that this would indeed be Rangers' year. But between them and their first trophy stood their fiercest and most deadly rivals – Celtic!

Rangers had won the first of their Old Firm duels at the end of August, but they knew that the champions were thirsting for revenge. But, as the game approached, Souness, still to make his debut against the Parkhead team was injured. He forced himself into a comeback against Boavista in the first leg UEFA Cup tie, but had to limp from the field in the first half. For the next few days

Left: The initial strike force of last season – Colin West and Ally McCoist, once team-mates at Sunderland. Unhappily West damaged his knee against East Fife

Right: Graham Roberts – the man who brought the title Rangers' way

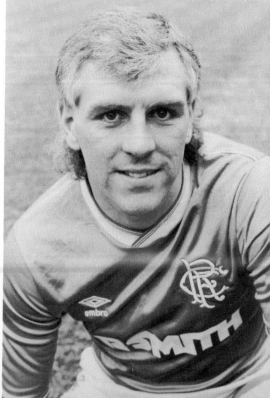

It's another international team clash – this time Aberdeen's Willie Miller moves in to tackle McCoist as the Ibrox man prepares to shoot

the player-boss fought to be ready . . . issuing daily bulletins which suggested he would be in his place ready for the Celtic challenge.

It was only after the game, a game which boiled over in fury and controversy, that Souness revealed that he had never had a chance of playing. All he had done was try to keep Celtic guessing as to his intentions. Derek Ferguson took over and was outstanding as Rangers battled their way to a 2–1 win.

Referee David Syme was heavily criticized by Celtic afterwards because of a penalty given to Rangers near the end of the match. But pictures in this book show without doubt that Parkhead captain Roy Aitken was holding Terry Butcher's jersey as the pair jostled for position in the penalty box.

Earlier Iain Durrant had scored the opener and Celtic boss Davie Hay admitted later: 'We always seem to be on the receiving end from him. . . .' Then there was an equalizer from Brian McClair, and the game was moving towards extra time in front of a huge Sunday afternoon crowd of 74,000 when the deadlock was broken. Syme gave the penalty, Davie Cooper, the spot-kick expert, sent it past Pat Bonner and Rangers were on their way to their first major trophy under the management of Graeme

The Hampden opener in the Skol Cup Final from Iain Durrant, on the left of the picture turning away with his arms raised

Brian McClair shoots from just inside the penalty box and Chris Woods, off his line, is beaten by the shot for Celtic's equalizer

Left: The start of the penalty incident with Roy Aitken clearly holding Terry Butcher's jersey . . .

Right: How could there be any doubt – Butcher has almost lost his jersey by this time and the penalty was given

Souness. The game ended in bitterness, with Mo Johnston being ordered off and Celtic protesting bitterly over the penalty award, but the camera doesn't lie. Davie Syme was right.

A week later Rangers had to go to Celtic Park in a League game, and a goal from Ally McCoist, that man again, gave them a 1–1 draw with the reigning champions.

Celtic, however, were still ahead in the Premier League race – a position they were to hold until late in the season. A shock defeat at home from Motherwell after returning from a victory in Boavista underlined how Rangers were still liable to fall victims to the sucker punch. Souness knew he had to change that if his team were to be champions. And, so, he began the moves which were to bring teak-tough Graham Roberts from Spurs to line up alongside Terry Butcher at the heart of the Rangers defence.

Later Souness was to admit: 'When I signed Roberts I knew that we could go on to take the title. It was the last piece of the jigsaw at the back. I had to have things right there. That was my major aim.

'It's why I went for Chris Woods, for Terry Butcher and then

for Graham Roberts. Being secure in defence is the mark of champions. Robbo was so important, arriving when he did. . . .'

The first game for the one-time Spurs star was on 27 December against Dundee United at Ibrox. More than 42,000 fans saw him settle in magnificently – and he followed that a few days later with an immaculate display against Celtic when Rangers repeated their 2–0 win over the Tannadice team in front of a capacity Ibrox crowd. Robert Fleck and Ally McCoist shared the goals in the Old Firm game but Souness was the star. He was the midfield puppet master, controlling every move, dictating the pace and the pattern of the game. Personally I had never seen a Rangers player dominate an Old Firm game so much since the days of Jim Baxter more than twenty years earlier!

It was a virtuoso performance, and it started Rangers on the run which was to finally bring them the championship. Until they met Celtic again in April at Parkhead, Rangers were not to lose a Premier League match.

There was that historic hiccup against Hamilton when Adrian Sprott scored to put himself into the record books alongside Sammy Reid. It was almost twenty years to the day since that Berwick Rangers Cup win over the Ibrox side when Reid scored. Now it was Sprott, and Rangers' embarrassment was complete because it had happened on their own ground.

But Roberts had added solidity to the defence and the younger players were gaining in confidence, and all the time they whittled away at the nine-point lead Celtic had enjoyed around Christmas. And Celtic themselves began to slip. Points were dropped, form became patchy and Rangers with Souness driving them ruthlessly took on the look of champions. That look remained with them until the last edgy days of the long, long season. Then they developed the nervousness which had proved fatal to Celtic . . . but it was never going to be enough to allow the Parkhead team to overtake them at the top. The iron discipline and the complete professionalism which Souness had brought to the defence was to make sure of that.

But there were other factors too, which helped the Ibrox men take the title. The form and growing mastery in midfield of Derek Ferguson and Iain Durrant. Ferguson was able to deputize for his boss on many occasions and the team rarely faltered – that is praise indeed for the youngster!

Durrant, of course, was able to score vital goals in vital games,

Ally McCoist has Scotland team-mate Dave Narey of Dundee United under pressure in a Rangers attack

Above: Defensive giants, Terry Butcher and Chris Woods – here the skipper congratulates Woods after his record-breaking number of shut-outs

Right: Scotland star Davie Cooper tries to go past Aberdeen's Brian Grant – Cooper had his best season in years

such as one against Celtic in the League win at Ibrox and another against them at Hampden in the Skol Cup Final. Then there were the strikers – McCoist and Fleck. . . . McCoist was always first choice as front man and he justified that with his scoring feats over the season. He scored thirty-five goals during the season and powered his way into the Scotland team ahead of a crowd of big name rivals for the striking positions.

Above: Phil Boersma, the Rangers physio, yells instructions from the dug-out

Right: Robert Fleck shows the determination which kept him in the first team as he battles against Fraser Wishart of Motherwell

Fleck appeared after Colin West had been injured and he remained in the first team. Yet, at the start of the season, it looked as if he would be leaving the club. Instead, though, he saw his chance and fought his way to becoming a regular. His goals helped enormously. He managed twenty-one first-team goals and over the season he scored *four* hat-tricks. One of them was in Europe against the Finnish team Ilves Tampere, the others in the League

against Clydebank, Falkirk and the poor Bankies again. It was an amazing season for the chunky forward who brought Jimmy Millar to mind for so many of the older fans.

Then there was Davie Cooper, so much more consistent than he had been in previous years, relishing the atmosphere, loving the service he was getting as Souness plied him with glorious passes.

All of these were backed by a defensive team as good as any in Britain, and with a new-found belief in themselves that helped the older Rangers players towards the title which had eluded them for nine years. It was their form against the top teams, too, which proved them as Souness stressed 'the best team in the country'.

Against Celtic they took five points from a possible eight.

Against Dundee United they took the same number of points. Against Aberdeen they took four points.

And against Hearts they managed seven points!

It was the way they dealt with the challenge from the top teams which was so impressive over the season. And, then, too, their lapses were fewer. Where they once failed to be convincing against lesser teams, this time round they tended to dominate except for the very occasional mistakes. Motherwell at Ibrox was one, Hamilton in the Scottish Cup was another.

If there was a major blow then it came from that Hamilton match. Souness still says it was the 'worst day of his life'. And also, perhaps, at the way they went out of Europe against the organized but scarcely brilliant Borussia Moenchengladbach.

If Souness had been fit to play in the first leg at Ibrox. . . .

If Graham Roberts had been signed early enough to have played in Europe. . . .

If the team had had just a little more experience. . . .

So it goes on. Personally, I feel the Souness factor was the main one. If the player-boss had been fit for both legs then Borussia would have been beaten. And Souness would have had a major challenge in Europe progressing alongside his charge for the championship!

Since then, of course, he has strengthened the team, and will go on doing so as long as he is manager at Ibrox. Souness will not sit back to enjoy *one* championship victory. Or *one* Skol Cup win. He will want more. And he will want to prove just how much his team can improve. The restless ambition which drove him to ask for a transfer from Spurs when he was a teenager, which saw him go on to Liverpool from Middlesbrough and then on to Sampdoria still burns as strongly. He intends Rangers to be the best. He won't rest until he is satisfied they are. . . .

And, even then, he will be looking for improvements. That is the way of the man!